DINOSAUR NUMBERS

PAUL STICKLAND

STERLING CHILDREN'S BOOKS
New York

STERLING CHILDREN'S BOOKS
New York

An Imprint of Sterling Publishing
387 Park Avenue South
New York, NY 10016

STERLING CHILDREN'S BOOKS and the distinctive
Sterling Children's Books logo are trademarks of Sterling Publishing Co., Inc.

Originally published 2010 in board book format by Sterling Publishing Company, Inc.,
387 Park Avenue South, New York, NY 10016.
New material © 2010 by Paul Stickland. Includes material previously published in *Dinosaur Colors and Numbers:
A Dinosaur Flip Book* by Backpack Books, New York, NY, by arrangement with Ragged Bears Publishing Ltd.,
Milborne Wick, Sherborne Dorset DT9 4PW England, and © 2005 by Paul Stickland.

Sterling ISBN 978-1-4549-1028-2

Distributed in Canada by Sterling Publishing
c/o Canadian Manda Group, 165 Dufferin Street
Toronto, Ontario, Canada M6K 3H6

For information about custom editions, special sales, and premium and corporate purchases,
please contact Sterling Special Sales at 800-805-5489 or specialsales@sterlingpublishing.com.

Manufactured in China
Lot #:
2 4 6 8 10 9 7 5 3 1
11/13

www.sterlingpublishing.com/kids

This book belongs to:

One

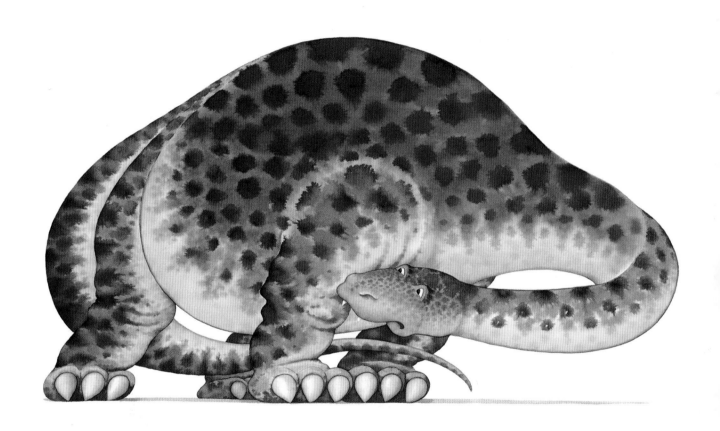

One big dinosaur standing all alone.

Two

Two hungry dinosaurs biting on some bones.

Three

Three jolly dinosaurs having lots of fun.

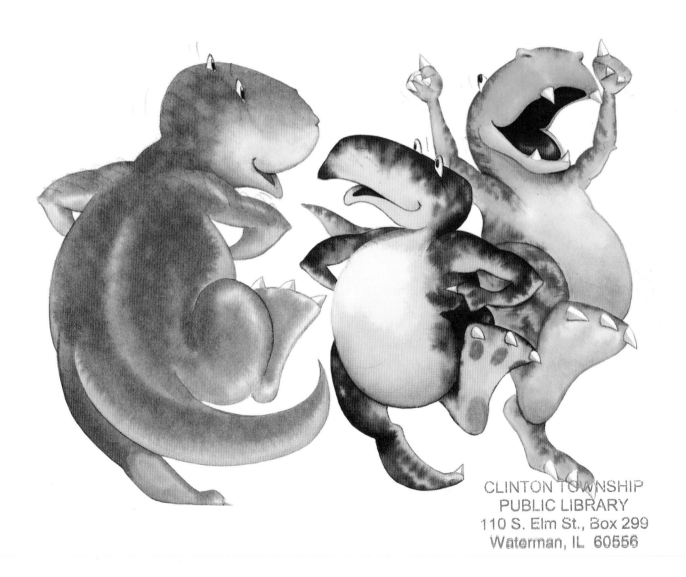

Four

Four fit dinosaurs going for a run.

Five

Five fat dinosaurs skipping along.

Six

Six happy dinosaurs singing a song.

Seven

Seven messy dinosaurs needing to get clean.

Eight

Eight playful dinosaurs trying to look mean.

Nine

Nine naughty dinosaurs hiding in a tree.

10

Ten

Ten terrific dinosaurs, happy as can be!

Also available from Sterling:

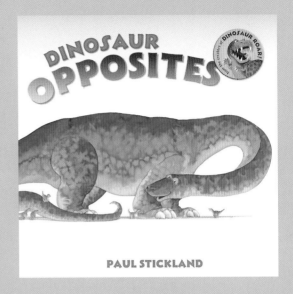

978-1-4549-1029-9

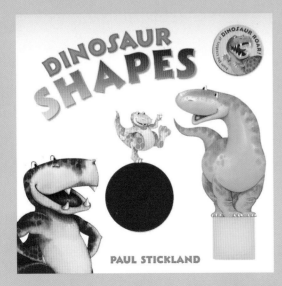

978-1-4549-1027-5

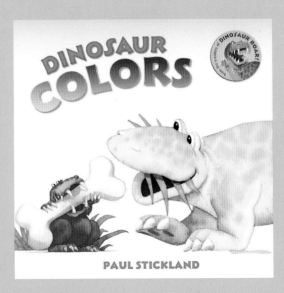

978-1-4027-9237-3